T0112581

FILL IN THE BLANK BUBBLE WITH **YOUR OWN** INTRODUCTION.

A Little Rockin' Book
WONDER BOY

THE D BY NUMBERS

HOPE
HOPE

AIR KAGE
KG
KG

TENACIOUS D

69
Br
eaking
69
Ga
ss

PLAYJACK
JACK TELLS ALL
"I always had perfect nipples."
FEAST YOUR EYES
$6.69
JANUARY / 94
SPECIAL DOUBLE-SIZED ISSUE
666281969 69

PLAYKYLE
FEAST YOUR EYES
$6.69
JANUARY / 94
KYLE OPENS UP
"Everybody wanted to play my flute. It was crazy!"
SPECIAL DOUBLE-SIZED ISSUE
6661419606969

TENACIOUS D

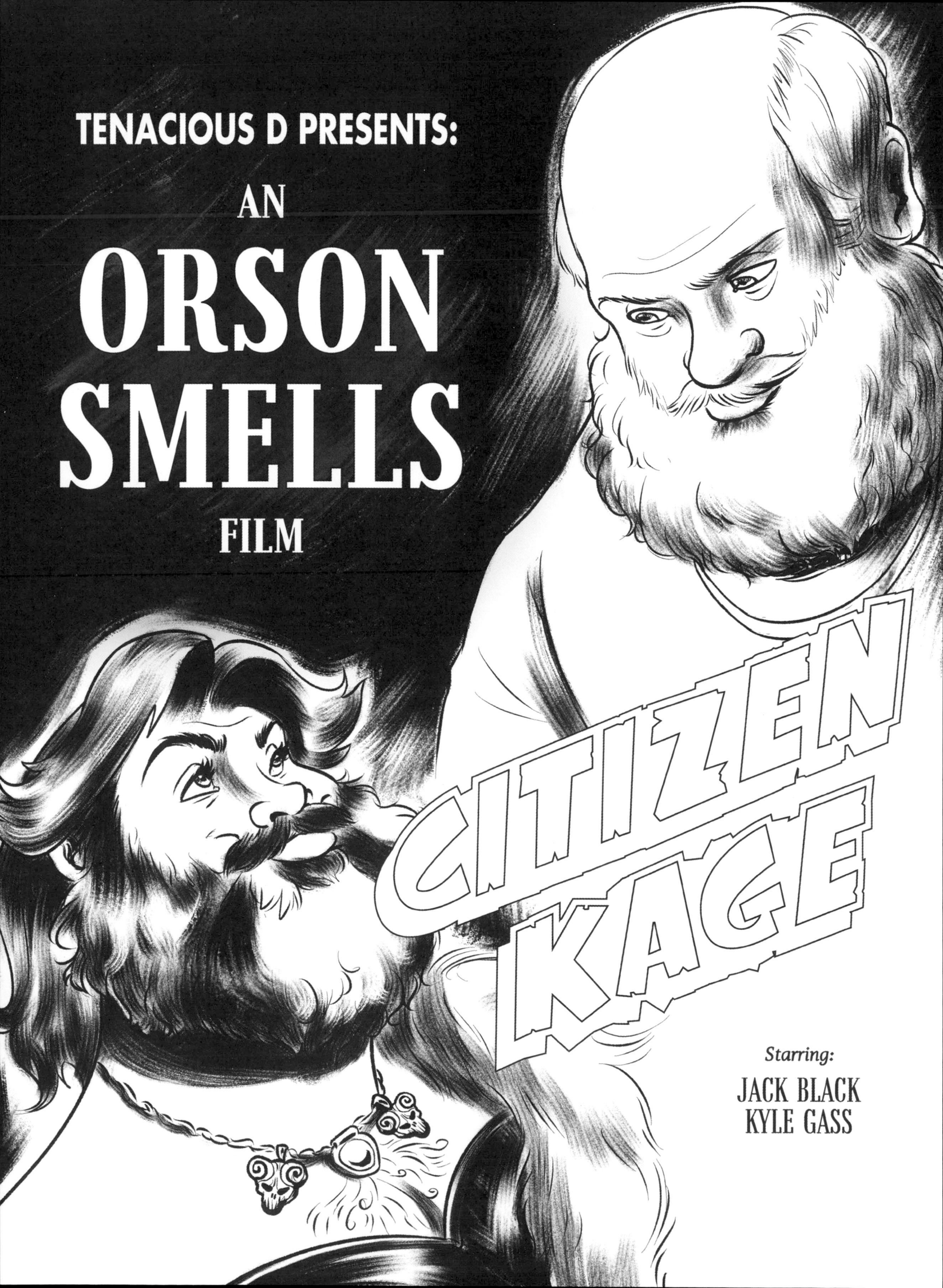
TENACIOUS D PRESENTS:
AN
ORSON
SMELLS
FILM
CITIZEN
KAGE
Starring:
JACK BLACK
KYLE GASS

MERRY
XMAS
from the D

Happy
Hanukkah
from the D!

COCKZILLA VS.
TENACIOUS D

ÇA OUT

The Motherfuckin'

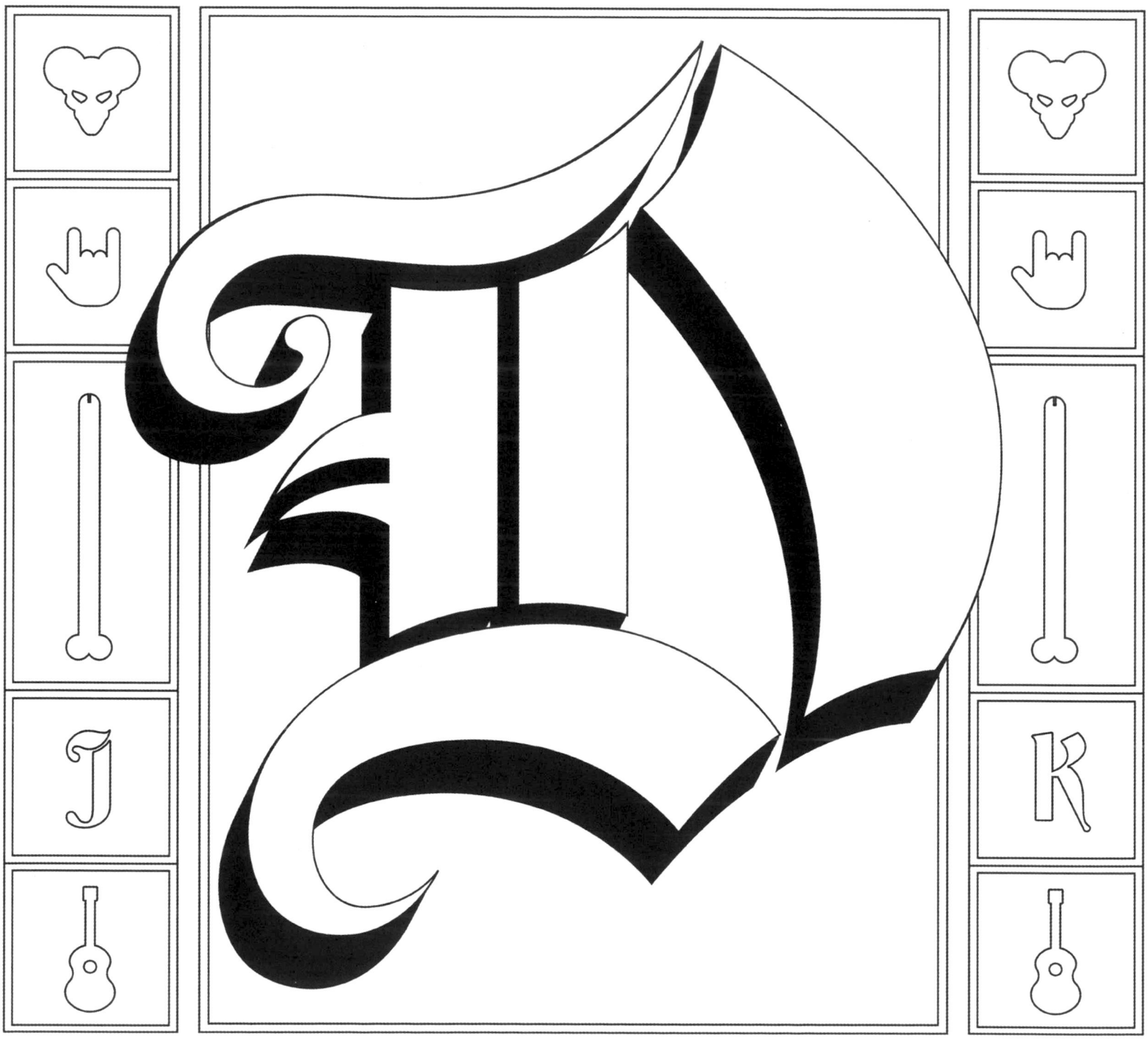

Jack Black • Kyle Gass

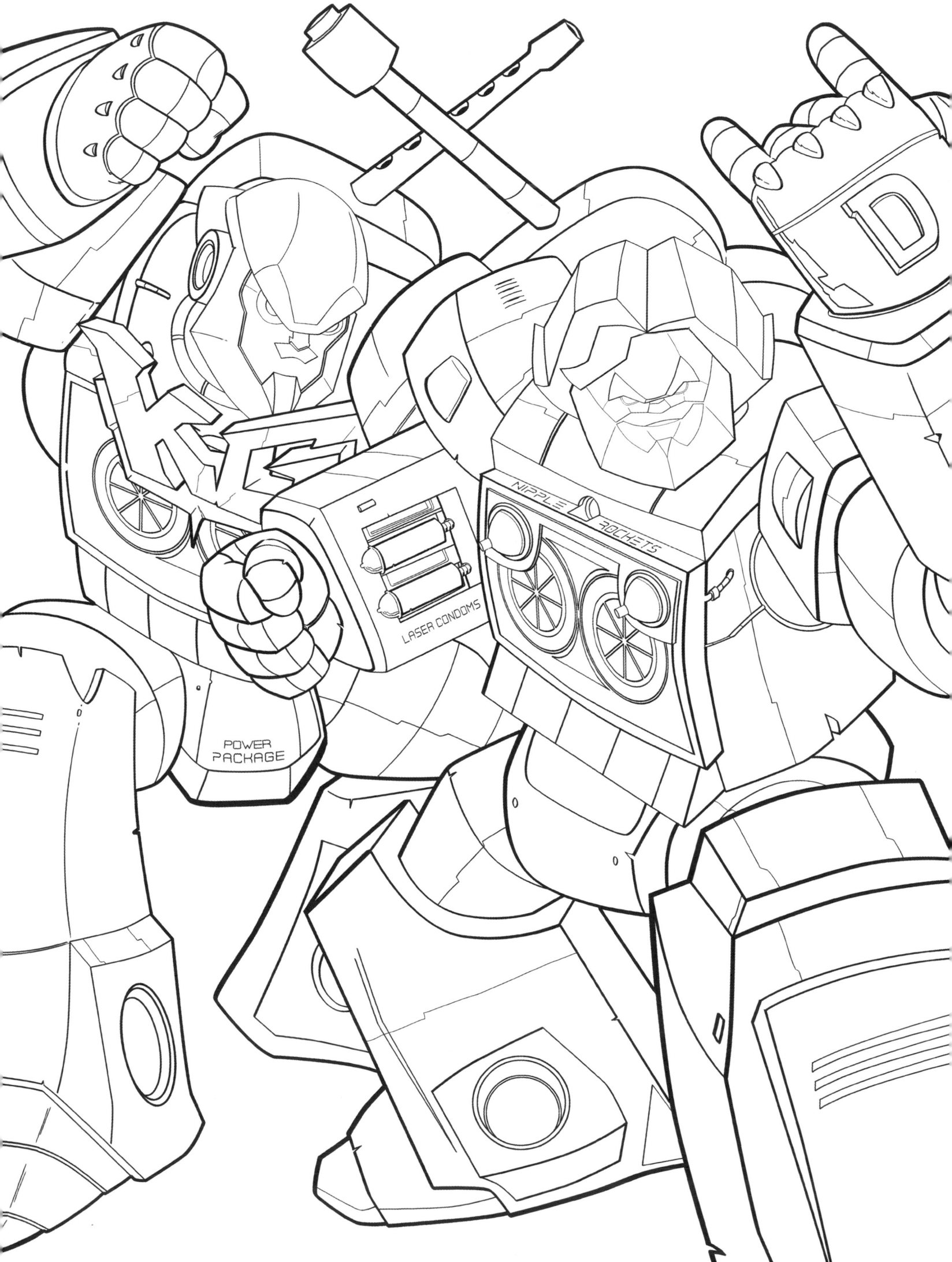
NIPPLE ROCKETS
LASER CONDOMS
POWER PACKAGE

CALIFORNIA
THE ROAD IS FUCKING HARD
Map Issued By
LUCIFER'S TOURIST BUREAU
Venice Beach, California

JACK
THE
BARBARIAN

Greetings
from
KICKAPOO
UNITED STATES OF AMERICA
MONSTER MASH!

MONSTER MASH!
MONSTER MASH!
MONSTER MASH!
MONSTER MASH!
MONSTER MASH!
MONSTER MASH!
MONSTER MASH!
MONSTER MASH!
MONSTER MASH!
MONSTER MASH!

JACK
SCORE:1026
KYLE
SCORE:2006
Gasstendo
Official
Gasstendo
Seal
SUPER GASSTENDO
ENTERTAINMENT SYSTEM

TENACIOUS
D&D
POST-
APOCALYPTO
EDITION

CAT
FOOD

BURNING
HOT WINGS

THE DAY AFTER
BURNING
HOT WINGS

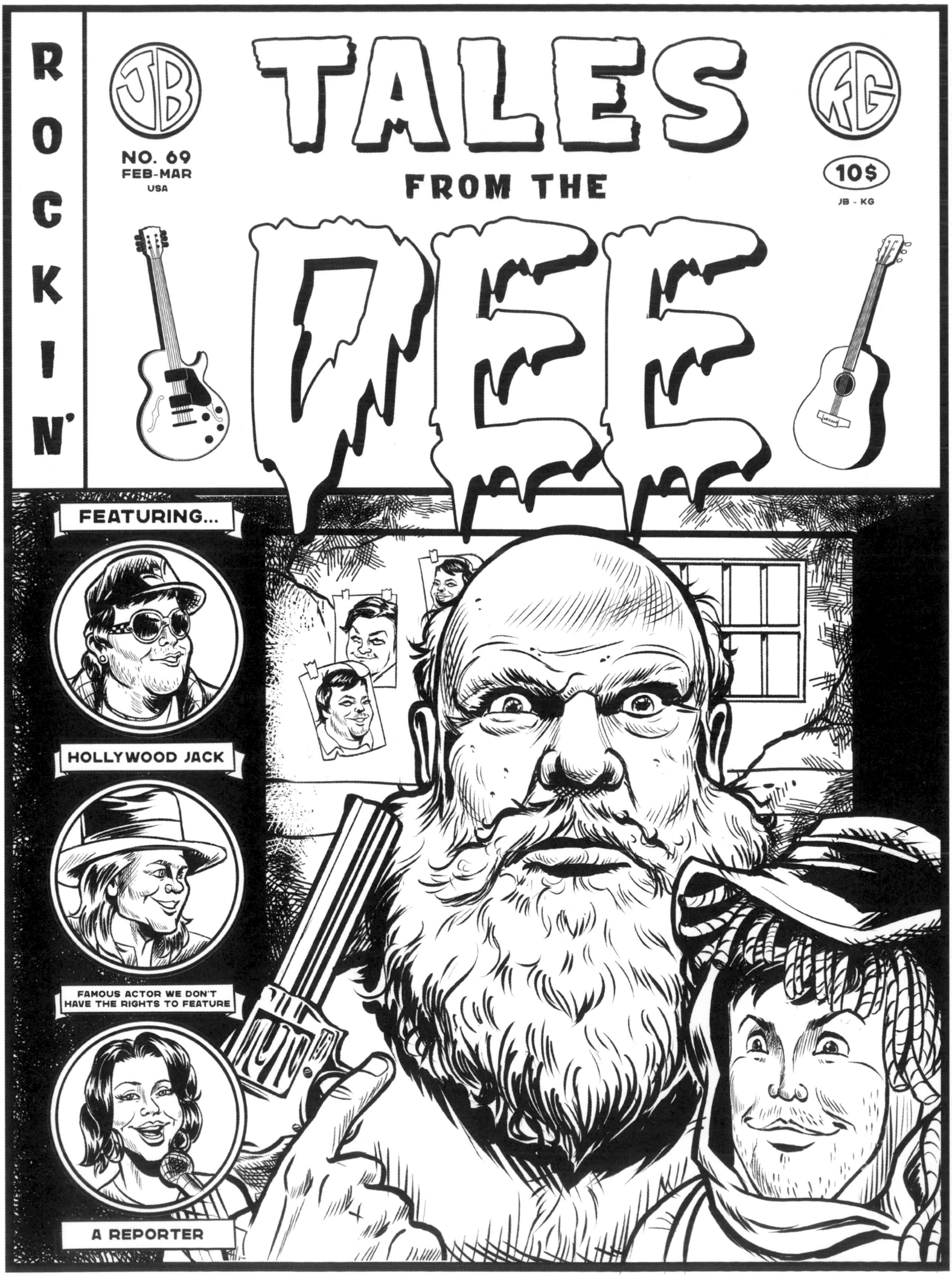
ROCKIN'
JB
NO. 69
FEB-MAR
USA
TALES
FROM THE
DEE
KG
10$
JB - KG
FEATURING...
HOLLYWOOD JACK
FAMOUS ACTOR WE DON'T HAVE THE RIGHTS TO FEATURE
A REPORTER

JBKGTDXXX

GASSHALEN

JBKGTDXXX

START
END

JB
TENACIOUS D
D
records
KG

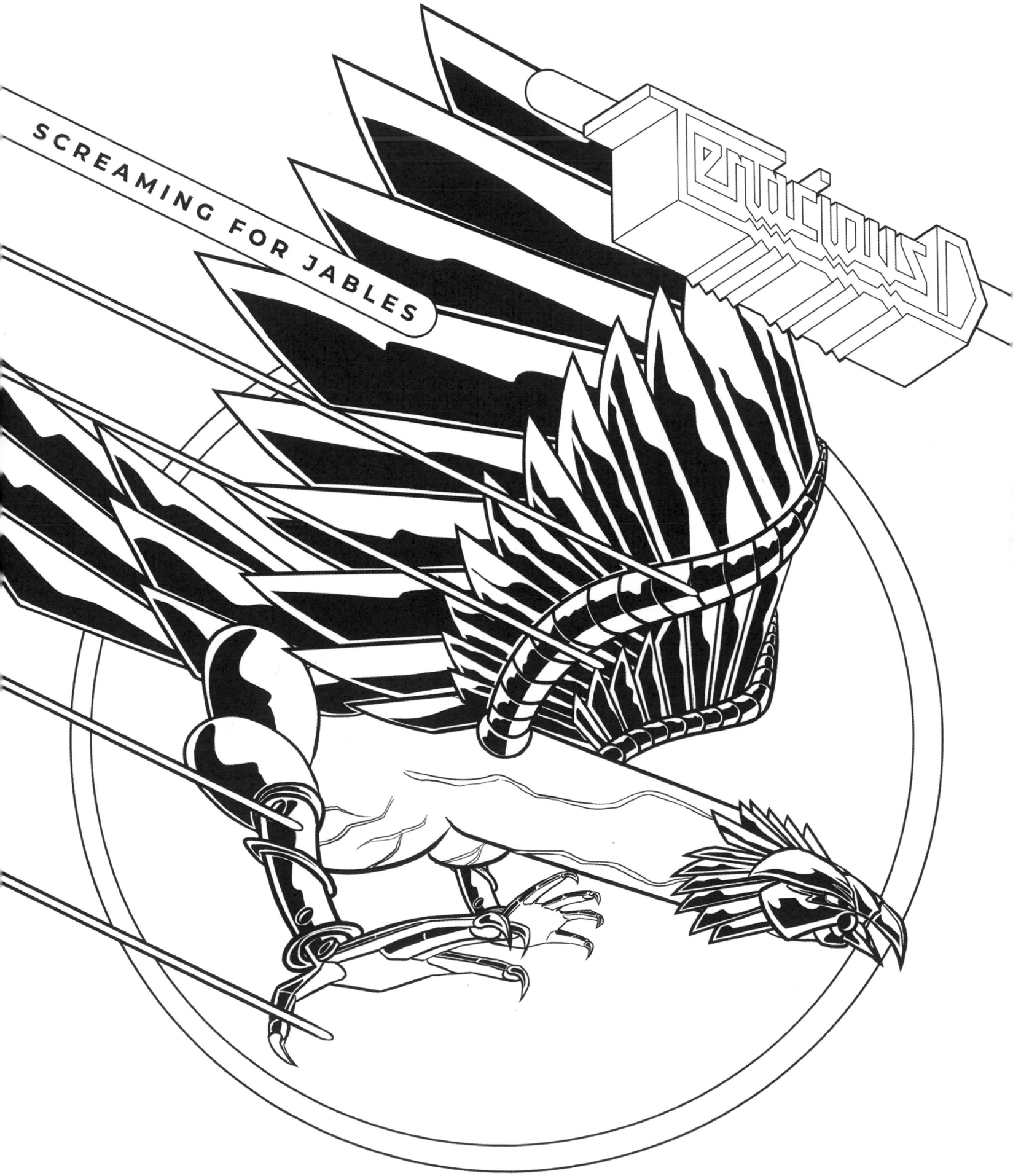
SCREAMING FOR JABLES
Envious

EXIT

TENACIOUS D WARP

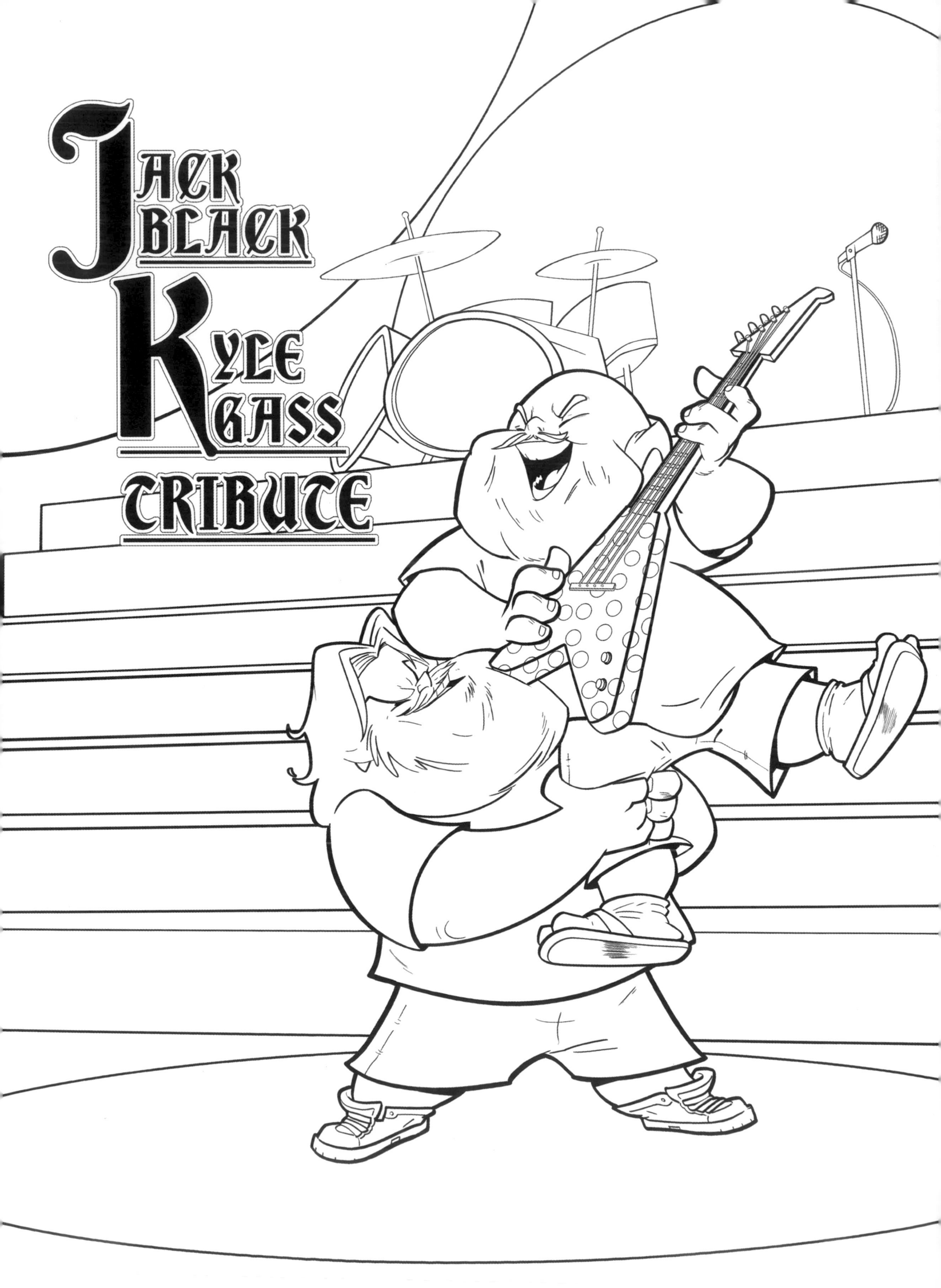
JACK BLACK
KYLE GASS
TRIBUTE

TENACIOUS D

THE SEXYPROG SOUNDS OF

Kyle Gass

2 Drain it.
1 Bite off just the tip of the burrito.
3 Let the chunks fall on a bed of chips.
JACK BLACK'S
DORITO BURRITO
4 Stuff chips into the hole.
5 Enjoy delicious burrito satchel filled with crunchy chips.

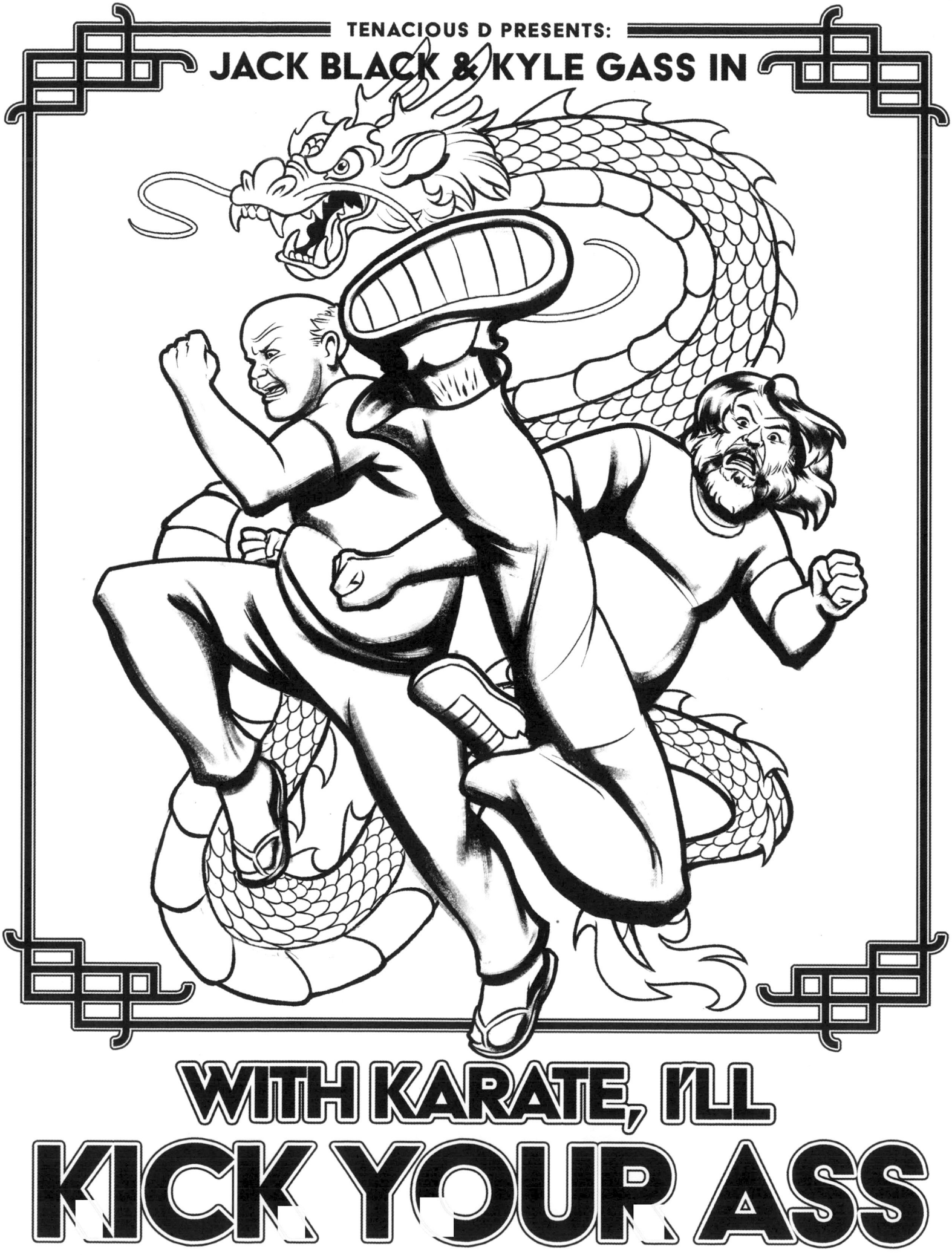
TENACIOUS D PRESENTS:
JACK BLACK & KYLE GASS IN
WITH KARATE, I'LL
KICK YOUR ASS

TENACIOUS
D

JABLES FOR PRESIDENT
THE GREATEST CANDIDATE IN THE WORLD
KAGE FOR PRESIDENT
I LIKE POPSICLES

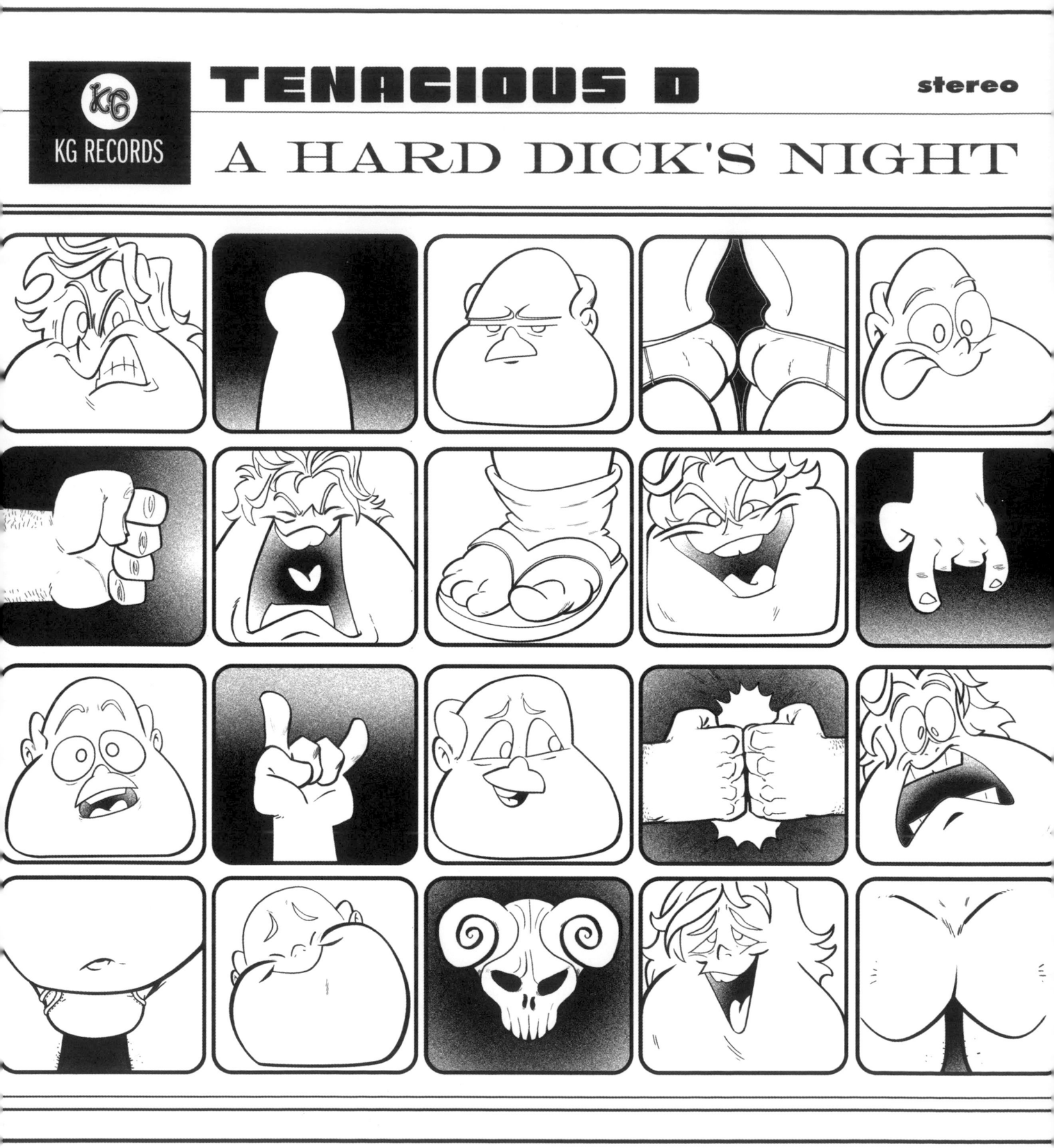
KG
KG RECORDS
TENACIOUS D
stereo
A HARD DICK'S NIGHT

A FILM BY GASSERGIO KYLEONE
THE SEARCH FOR INSPIRADO
JEF FAN JEFF - MARIA SASQUATCH

MUTHERFUKIN JABLES

THE ROBOT

CHIN

Post-Apocalypto
Take us into space
DDDP
DDDP
2001

VENICE BEACH'S
THE BEARDED
MERMAID
AND THE SHELL OF DESTINY

BREAKING NEWS
SEISMIC ACTIVITY IN WESTERN SPRINGS, NEW ZEALAND!
LIVE
TD

TENACIOUS D PICTURES PRESENTS:

The Podfather

STARRING

JACK BLACK AND KYLE GASS

AND

JR REED RONNIE JAMES DIO MEAT LOAF TROY GENTILE BEN STILLER DAVE GROHL

DIRECTED BY:

LIAM LYNCH

WRITTEN BY:

JACK BLACK, KYLE GASS AND LIAM LYNCH

D PRODUCTIONS

LEAD BELLY
ELVIS
LED ZEPPELIN
RIGHT SAID FRED
THE BEATLES
THE GRATEFUL DEAD
FREDDIE MERCURY
ROCK 'N' ROLL

TENACIOUS D

D NOTE

SIMPLY JAZZ

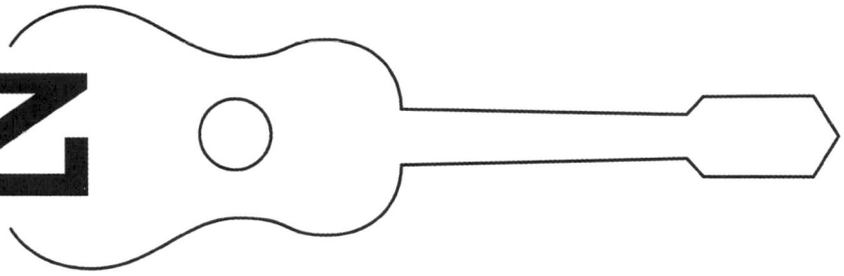

TD6JB6KG6

THE METAL

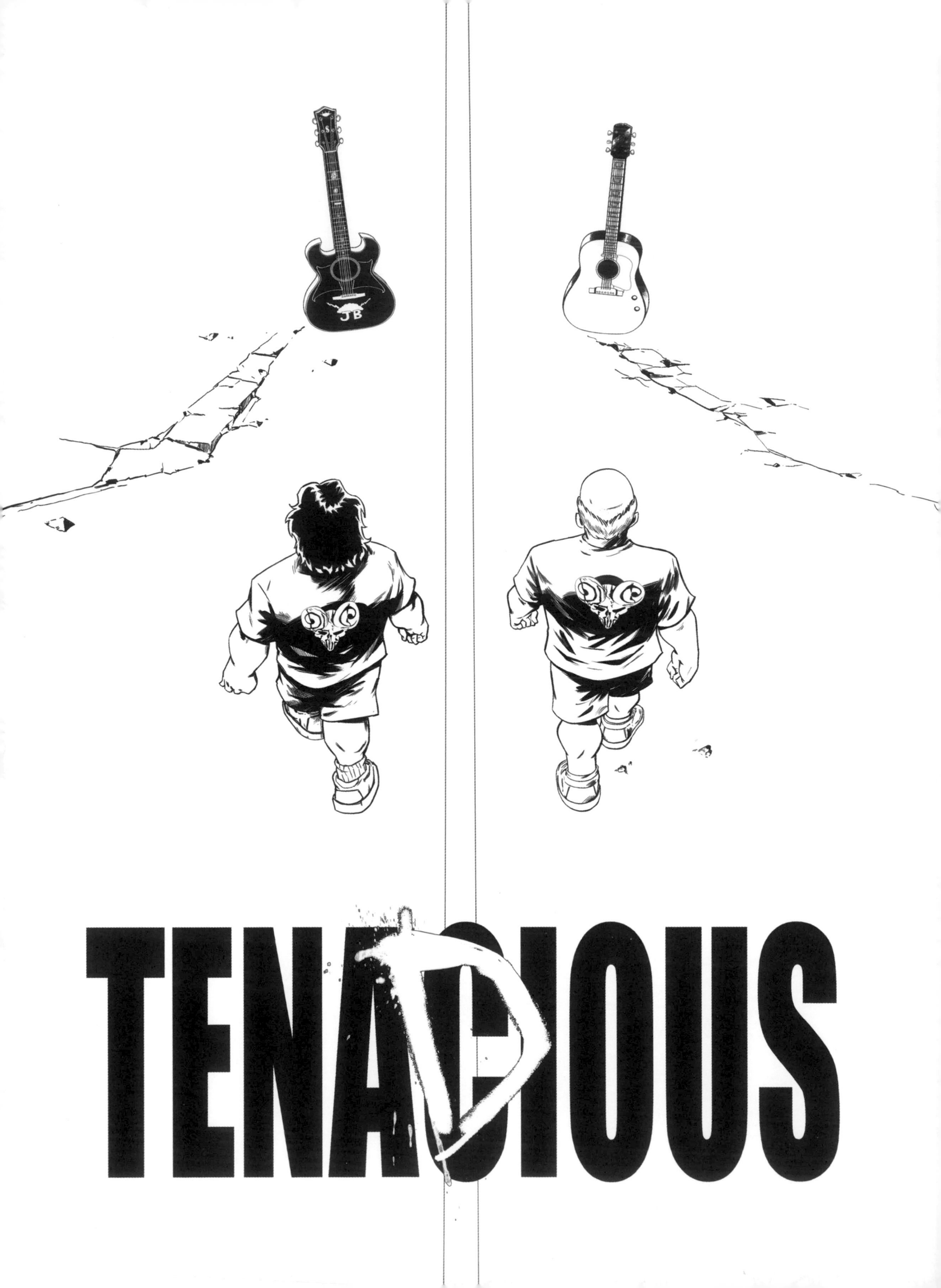
JB
TENACIOUS

START
END

JACK
KYLE

D·D'S

TD